Healing Journeys

A Guided Journal to Overcoming Trauma Through Faith and Wholeness

Adapted from the book: "Overcoming Trauma through Christ"

Discover Your Path to Healing and Wholeness with Daily Prompts and Reflections

This journal belongs to the

| |
| |

Areas I need healing:

I am dedicating myself to:

I forgive others for:

I forgive myself for:

My prayer is:

Introduction

This guided journal is designed to accompany readers on their healing journey, offering daily prompts and reflections to help them overcome trauma through faith and wholeness. With powerful scripture passages, insightful prompts, and space for personal reflection, this journal is the perfect tool for anyone seeking to find peace and healing in the midst of pain. From cultivating forgiveness and compassion, to sharing your story and finding purpose in your pain, each daily prompt offers actionable strategies and inspiring insights for moving forward in your healing journey. Whether you are struggling with the aftermath of abuse, loss, or any other form of trauma, this journal will offer you the support and guidance you need to navigate your path toward wholeness and hope.

These journal questions, prompts, prayers, and scriptures will help you reflect on your experiences and beliefs and to engage in deeper self-exploration as you work through your own healing journey. They encourage readers to consider your relationship with God, the role of forgiveness and compassion in your live, and the benefits of sharing your story with others.

Psalm 34:18 - *"The Lord is close to the brokenhearted and saves those who are crushed in spirit."*

Journal Prompts

Think about a traumatic experience in your life that you haven't fully processed or healed from. Write about what happened, how it made you feel, and any lingering effects it has had on you.

Reflect on a time when you felt God's presence in the midst of a difficult situation. How did you experience his love and comfort?:

_____

_____

_____

_____

_____

_____

_____

_____

_____

_____

_____

_____

_____

_____

_____

_____

Write a letter to God expressing any anger, frustration, or sadness you feel about the trauma you've experienced. Ask for his help in processing your emotions and finding healing

Consider the role that forgiveness plays in your healing journey. Are there people in your life that you need to forgive? Write about your experience of extending forgiveness to someone who has hurt you, or the process of seeking forgiveness from someone you've hurt.

List of People I need to forgive:

_____

_____

_____

_____

_____

_____

_____

_____

_____

_____

_____

_____

Reflection:

Reflect on the idea of "sharing your story." Why is it important to share your experience with others, and what benefits have you experienced as a result of sharing your story? Write about a time when you shared your story with someone else. What was their response? How did it feel to open up and be vulnerable?

Think about any fears or anxieties you have about the future, and write a prayer asking God to give you strength and courage to move forward.

Consider how you can use your experience to help others who are going through similar struggles. Write about any ideas you have for serving and supporting others who are dealing with trauma.

Reflect on the ways that God has been faithful to you throughout your healing journey. Write a list of blessings and things you are grateful for.

What does the concept of "overcoming" mean to you? How do you define it in the context of your trauma?

Reflect on when you felt particularly close to God during your healing journey. What did that experience look and feel like?

How have your beliefs about God changed or evolved due to your trauma? Do you feel closer to God or further away from him?

Think about a time when you experienced a setback or relapse in your healing journey. How did you respond to it, and what did you learn from the experience?

What practices or habits have helped you to cope with the pain and trauma of your experience? Do you regularly do things that help you feel more grounded, centered, or connected to God?

What do you hope to gain from your healing journey? What are your goals, and how do you envision your life looking once you've fully processed and healed from your trauma?

30 days of prayers to overcome trauma:

Day 1: Heavenly Father, I come to you with a heavy heart, burdened by the trauma that I have experienced. Please grant me the strength and courage to face my pain and to trust in your love and care.	*Day 2:* Lord, I ask for your healing touch to come upon me today. Please soothe my pain and comfort me in my distress.
Day 3: Dear God, I am struggling to forgive those who have hurt me. Please help me to extend compassion and grace towards them, and to release the bitterness in my heart.	*Day 4:* Lord, I pray for your protection over me as I work through my healing journey. Shield me from any negative or harmful influences, and surround me with your love and light.
Day 5: Heavenly Father, I ask for your wisdom and guidance as I make decisions about my healing journey. Please help me to discern the path that is best for me, and to trust in your divine plan for my life.	*Day 6:* Lord, I pray for the strength to persevere through the challenges and setbacks that I may encounter on my healing journey. Please help me to stay grounded in your love and to trust in your promises.
Day 7: Dear God, I ask for your grace and compassion to flow through me as I work through my emotions and feelings. Please help me to offer myself the same kindness and understanding that I extend to others.	*Day 8:* Lord, I pray for your peace to fill my heart and mind today. Please help me to let go of my worries and anxieties, and to trust in your provision and care.

Day 9: Heavenly Father, I ask for your healing touch to come upon me today. Please restore my sense of safety and security, and help me to find peace in the midst of my trauma.	*Day 10:* Lord, I pray for the courage to share my story with others. Please help me to speak truthfully and authentically, and to offer hope and encouragement to those who may be struggling.
Day 11: Dear God, I ask for your strength to overcome any feelings of shame or guilt that may be holding me back. Please help me to see myself as you see me - loved, valued, and worthy.	*Day 12:* Lord, I pray for your mercy and grace to come upon me today. Please forgive me for any wrongs I have committed, and help me extend the same forgiveness to others.
Day 13: Heavenly Father, I ask for your healing touch to come upon me today. Please restore my self-worth and self-esteem, and help me see myself as you see me.	*Day 14:* Lord, I pray for your peace to guard my heart and mind today. Please help me to trust in your faithfulness and to rest in your presence.
Day 15: Dear God, I ask for your comfort and care to surround me today. Please help me to feel your loving embrace, and to know that I am not alone in my pain.	*Day 16:* Lord, I pray for your wisdom and discernment as I make decisions about my healing journey. Please help me to seek out the guidance and support that I need, and to trust in your leadership.

Day 17: Heavenly Father, I ask for your strength and perseverance to see me through the challenges of my healing journey. Please help me to keep my eyes fixed on you, and to trust in your promises.	***Day 18:*** Lord, I pray for your mercy and compassion to flow through me as I interact with others. Please help me to extend grace and kindness to those who may be struggling or hurting.
Day 19: Dear God, I ask for your presence to be with me as I process my emotions and feelings. Please help me to find the courage to face my pain, and to trust in your healing power.	***Day 20:*** Lord, I pray for your protection over me as I work through my trauma. Please shield me from any harmful influences, and surround me with your love and care.
Day 21: Heavenly Father, I ask for your peace to fill my heart and mind today. Please help me to let go of any fear or anxiety, and to trust in your unfailing love.	***Day 22:*** Lord, I pray for your healing touch to come upon me today. Please restore my sense of hope and optimism, and help me to believe that a brighter future is possible.
Day 23: Dear God, I ask for your wisdom and guidance as I navigate the ups and downs of my healing journey. Please help me to stay focused on you, and to trust in your goodness and faithfulness.	***Day 24:*** Lord, I pray for your grace and compassion to flow through me as I interact with others. Please help me to be patient and understanding, and to extend kindness to those who may be struggling.

Day 25: Heavenly Father, I ask for your strength and perseverance to see me through the challenges of my healing journey. Please help me to remain steadfast in my faith, and trust in your promises.	***Day 26:*** Lord, I pray for your mercy and forgiveness to come upon me today. Please help me to release any bitterness or resentment, and to extend grace to those who have hurt me.
Day 27: Dear God, I ask for your healing touch to come upon me today. Please restore my sense of purpose and meaning, and help me find joy amid my pain.	***Day 28:*** Lord, I pray for your peace to guard my heart and mind today. Please help me to let go of any worries or anxieties and to trust in your provision and care.
Day 29: Heavenly Father, I ask for your comfort and care to surround me today. Please help me to feel your loving embrace and to know that you are with me always.	***Day 30:*** Lord, I pray for your blessing and favor to be upon me as I continue on my healing journey. Please help me to walk in faith and hope, and to trust in your plans and purposes for my life. Amen.

30 daily activities to help you overcome trauma:

Day 1: Write a letter to God expressing your emotions and feelings about your trauma.	***Day 2:*** Write down three things you are grateful for today, no matter how small.
Day 3: Identify a healthy coping mechanism that works for you and practice it today.	***Day 4:*** Go for a walk outside and take notice of the beauty around you.
Day 5: Spend time meditating on a Bible verse that brings you comfort.	***Day 6:*** Reach out to someone who has supported you through your healing journey and express your gratitude.
Day 7: Make a list of things that bring you joy and try to incorporate one of them into your day.	***Day 8:*** Write about a time when you showed yourself compassion during a difficult moment.
Day 9: Connect with a trusted friend or therapist and share your thoughts and feelings about your trauma.	***Day 10:*** Identify a negative thought pattern that you want to challenge and replace it with a positive affirmation.
Day 11: Take a break from social media and spend time reading a book or doing an activity you enjoy.	***Day 12:*** Practice deep breathing exercises for 5 minutes and notice how it affects your body and mind.
Day 13: Write a letter to your younger self, offering comfort and support during a difficult time.	***Day 14:*** Identify a self-care activity that works for you and make time for it today.

Day 15: Connect with nature by hiking, gardening, or at the beach.	***Day 16:*** Write down three things you can do to cultivate a positive mindset.
Day 17: Practice mindfulness by focusing on the present moment and letting go of worries about the future.	***Day 18:*** Reach out to a support group or online community for individuals who have experienced trauma.
Day 19: Identify how you can serve others, and plan to put it into action.	***Day 20:*** Practice self-compassion by acknowledging your mistakes and offering yourself forgiveness.
Day 21: Spend time in prayer, asking God for strength, healing, and peace.	***Day 22:*** Write down three goals for your healing journey and make a plan to work towards them.
Day 23: Engage in a creative activity that allows you to express yourself and process your emotions.	***Day 24:*** Practice gratitude by making a list of things you are thankful for in your life.
Day 25: Identify a limiting belief that you hold about yourself and challenge it with evidence to the contrary.	***Day 26:*** Connect with a trusted friend or family member and express your appreciation for their support.
Day 27: Spend time in nature, either by going for a walk, hiking, or simply sitting and enjoying the outdoors.	***Day 28:*** Practice forgiveness by reflecting on a person or situation that has caused you pain and offering them forgiveness.

| *Day 29:* Write a letter to your future self, expressing your hopes and dreams for your healing journey. | *Day 30:* Reflect on the progress you've made in your healing journey and celebrate the growth and healing that has taken place. |

Scriptures

These scriptures can inspire you to have faith in the healing power of God. They remind us that our prayers offered in faith can lead to healing, and that Jesus often commended individuals for their faith when they received healing. They encourage us to believe that God rewards those who earnestly seek him and that he can heal our physical, emotional, and spiritual wounds.

Additionally, they remind us that the ultimate source of our healing is through the wounds of Jesus Christ, who bore our sins and brought us peace. Here are some Scriptures that can offer comfort, hope, and healing to those who have experienced trauma:

Psalm 34:18 - "The Lord is close to the brokenhearted and saves those who are crushed in spirit."

Isaiah 41:10 - "So do not fear, for I am with you; do not be dismayed, for I am your God. I will strengthen you and help you; I will uphold you with my righteous right hand."

Psalm 23:4 - "Even though I walk through the darkest valley, I will fear no evil, for you are with me; your rod and your staff, they comfort me."

Matthew 11:28-30 - "Come to me, all you who are weary and burdened, and I will give you rest. Take my yoke upon you and learn from me, for I am gentle and humble in heart, and you will find rest for your souls. For my yoke is easy and my burden is light."

Romans 8:28 - "And we know that in all things God works for the good of those who love him, who have been called according to his purpose."

Isaiah 53:4-5 - "Surely he took up our pain and bore our suffering, yet we considered him punished by God, stricken by him, and afflicted. But he was pierced for our transgressions, he was crushed for our iniquities; the punishment that brought us peace was on him, and by his wounds we are healed."

Philippians 4:6-7 - "Do not be anxious about anything, but in every situation, by prayer and petition, with thanksgiving, present your requests to God. And the peace of God, which transcends all understanding, will guard your hearts and your minds in Christ Jesus."

2 Corinthians 1:3-4 *-* "Praise be to the God and Father of our Lord Jesus Christ, the Father of compassion and the God of all comfort, who comforts us in all our troubles, so that we can comfort those in any trouble with the comfort we ourselves receive from God."

Psalm 147:3 *-* "He heals the brokenhearted and binds up their wounds."

Isaiah 61:1 *-* "The Spirit of the Sovereign Lord is on me, because the Lord has anointed me to proclaim good news to the poor. He has sent me to bind up the brokenhearted, to proclaim freedom for the captives and release from darkness for the prisoners."

These scriptures can offer hope, comfort, and guidance to those who have experienced trauma, reminding them that they are not alone, and that God is always present to heal and restore.

Here are some Scriptures that can offer comfort, hope, and healing to those who have experienced trauma:

Psalm 34:18 *-* "The Lord is close to the brokenhearted and saves those who are crushed in spirit."

Isaiah 41:10 - "So do not fear, for I am with you; do not be dismayed, for I am your God. I will strengthen you and help you; I will uphold you with my righteous right hand."

Psalm 23:4 - "Even though I walk through the darkest valley, I will fear no evil, for you are with me; your rod and your staff, they comfort me."

Matthew 11:28-30 - "Come to me, all you who are weary and burdened, and I will give you rest. Take my yoke upon you and learn from me, for I am gentle and humble in heart, and you will find rest for your souls. For my yoke is easy and my burden is light."

Romans 8:28 - "And we know that in all things God works for the good of those who love him, who have been called according to his purpose."

Isaiah 53:4-5 - "Surely he took up our pain and bore our suffering, yet we considered him punished by God, stricken by him, and afflicted. But he was pierced for our transgressions, he was crushed for our iniquities; the punishment that brought us peace was on him, and by his wounds we are healed."

Philippians 4:6-7 - "Do not be anxious about anything, but in every situation, by prayer and petition, with thanksgiving, present your requests to God. And the peace of God, which transcends all understanding, will guard your hearts and your minds in Christ Jesus."

2 Corinthians 1:3-4 - "Praise be to the God and Father of our Lord Jesus Christ, the Father of compassion and the God of all comfort, who comforts us in all our troubles, so that we can comfort those in any trouble with the comfort we ourselves receive from God."

Psalm 147:3 - "He heals the brokenhearted and binds up their wounds."

Isaiah 61:1 - "The Spirit of the Sovereign Lord is on me, because the Lord has anointed me to proclaim good news to the poor. He has sent me to bind up the brokenhearted, to proclaim freedom for the captives and release from darkness for the prisoners."

Philippians 4:13 - "I can do all things through Christ who strengthens me."

Psalm 121:1-2 *-* "I lift up my eyes to the hills. From where does my help come? My help comes from the Lord, who made heaven and earth."

Isaiah 43:2 *-* "When you pass through the waters, I will be with you; and through the rivers, they shall not overwhelm you; when you walk through fire you shall not be burned, and the flame shall not consume you."

Romans 8:28 *-* "And we know that in all things God works for the good of those who love him, who have been called according to his purpose."

James 1:2-4 *-* "Consider it pure joy, my brothers and sisters, whenever you face trials of many kinds, because you know that the testing of your faith produces perseverance. Let perseverance finish its work so that you may be mature and complete, not lacking anything."

2 Corinthians 12:9-10 *-* "But he said to me, 'My grace is sufficient for you, for my power is made perfect in weakness.' Therefore I will boast all the more gladly about my weaknesses, so that Christ's power may rest on me. That is why, for Christ's sake, I delight in weaknesses, in insults, in hardships, in persecutions, in difficulties. For when I am weak, then I am strong."

Hebrews 11:1 - "Now faith is confidence in what we hope for and assurance about what we do not see."

Colossians 3:13 - "Bear with each other and forgive one another if any of you has a grievance against someone. Forgive as the Lord forgave you."

Matthew 6:14-15 - "For if you forgive other people when they sin against you, your heavenly Father will also forgive you. But if you do not forgive others their sins, your Father will not forgive your sins."

Luke 6:37 - "Do not judge, and you will not be judged. Do not condemn, and you will not be condemned. Forgive, and you will be forgiven."

Ephesians 4:31-32 - "Get rid of all bitterness, rage and anger, brawling and slander, along with every form of malice. Be kind and compassionate to one another, forgiving each other, just as in Christ God forgave you."

Proverbs 17:9 - "Whoever would foster love covers over an offense, but whoever repeats the matter separates close friends."

1 Peter 3:8-9 - "Finally, all of you, be like-minded, be sympathetic, love one another, be compassionate and humble. Do not repay evil with evil or insult with insult. On the contrary, repay evil with blessing, because to this you were called so that you may inherit a blessing."

Psalm 103:8 - "The Lord is compassionate and gracious, slow to anger, abounding in love."

Romans 8:28 - "And we know that in all things God works for the good of those who love him, who have been called according to his purpose."

Psalm 34:18 - "The Lord is close to the brokenhearted and saves those who are crushed in spirit."

Isaiah 43:2 - "When you pass through the waters, I will be with you; and through the rivers, they shall not overwhelm you; when you walk through fire you shall not be burned, and the flame shall not consume you."

Psalm 23:4 - "Even though I walk through the darkest valley, I will fear no evil, for you are with me; your rod and your staff, they comfort me."

2 Corinthians 12:9-10 - "But he said to me, 'My grace is sufficient for you, for my power is made perfect in weakness.' Therefore I will boast all the more gladly about my weaknesses, so that Christ's power may rest on me. That is why, for Christ's sake, I delight in weaknesses, in insults, in hardships, in persecutions, in difficulties. For when I am weak, then I am strong."

Hebrews 12:1-2 - "Therefore, since we are surrounded by such a great cloud of witnesses, let us throw off everything that hinders and the sin that so easily entangles. And let us run with perseverance the race marked out for us, fixing our eyes on Jesus, the pioneer and perfecter of faith. For the joy set before him he endured the cross, scorning its shame, and sat down at the right hand of the throne of God."

James 1:12 - "Blessed is the one who perseveres under trial because, having stood the test, that person will receive the crown of life that the Lord has promised to those who love him."

Psalm 107:2 - "Let the redeemed of the Lord tell their story—those he redeemed from the hand of the foe."

2 Corinthians 1:3-4 - "Praise be to the God and Father of our Lord Jesus Christ, the Father of compassion and the God of all comfort, who comforts us in all our troubles, so that we can comfort those in any trouble with the comfort we ourselves receive from God."

Revelation 12:11 - "They triumphed over him by the blood of the Lamb and by the word of their testimony; they did not love their lives so much as to shrink from death."

Isaiah 43:10 - "You are my witnesses," declares the Lord, "and my servant whom I have chosen, so that you may know and believe me and understand that I am he."

Psalm 66:16 - "Come and hear, all you who fear God; let me tell you what he has done for me."

Mark 5:19 - "Go home to your own people and tell them how much the Lord has done for you, and how he has had mercy on you."

1 Peter 3:15 - "But in your hearts revere Christ as Lord.

Always be prepared to give an answer to everyone who asks you to give the reason for the hope that you have. But do this with gentleness and respect."

Philippians 3:13-14 - "Brothers and sisters, I do not consider myself yet to have taken hold of it. But one thing I do: Forgetting what is behind and straining toward what is ahead, I press on toward the goal to win the prize for which God has called me heavenward in Christ Jesus."

Isaiah 43:18-19 - "Forget the former things; do not dwell on the past. See, I am doing a new thing! Now it springs up; do you not perceive it? I am making a way in the wilderness and streams in the wasteland."

Proverbs 4:25-26 - "Let your eyes look straight ahead; fix your gaze directly before you. Give careful thought to the paths for your feet and be steadfast in all your ways."

Philippians 4:6-7 - "Do not be anxious about anything, but in every situation, by prayer and petition, with thanksgiving, present your requests to God. And the peace of God, which transcends all understanding, will guard your hearts and your minds in Christ Jesus."

Psalm 37:23-24 - "The Lord makes firm the steps of the one who delights in him; though he may stumble, he will not fall, for the Lord upholds him with his hand."

Romans 12:12 - "Be joyful in hope, patient in affliction, faithful in prayer."

Hebrews 12:1-2 - "Therefore, since we are surrounded by such a great cloud of witnesses, let us throw off everything that hinders and the sin that so easily entangles. And let us run with perseverance the race marked out for us, fixing our eyes on Jesus, the pioneer and perfecter of faith."

James 5:15 - "And the prayer offered in faith will make the sick person well; the Lord will raise them up. If they have sinned, they will be forgiven."

Mark 11:24 - "Therefore I tell you, whatever you ask for in prayer, believe that you have received it, and it will be yours."

Matthew 9:22 - "Jesus turned and saw her. 'Take heart, daughter,' he said, 'your faith has healed you.' And the woman was healed at that moment."

Hebrews 11:6 - "And without faith it is impossible to please God, because anyone who comes to him must believe that he exists and that he rewards those who earnestly seek him."

Psalm 147:3 - "He heals the brokenhearted and binds up their wounds."

Isaiah 53:5 - "But he was pierced for our transgressions, he was crushed for our iniquities; the punishment that brought us peace was on him, and by his wounds we are healed."

1 Peter 2:24 - "He himself bore our sins in his body on the cross, so that we might die to sins and live for righteousness; by his wounds you have been healed."

Prayers

Here are some prayers when dealing with trauma:

Prayer for Comfort:
Heavenly Father, I come to you today to ask for your comfort and peace to surround those dealing with trauma. Lord, you know the pain and hurt that they are feeling, and I pray that you would wrap your loving arms around them and bring them a sense of calm. Please help them to feel your presence and to know that you are with them through difficult times. In Jesus' name, I pray. Amen.

Prayer for Healing:
Dear God, I pray for those dealing with trauma and ask that you bring them healing. Lord, you are the great physician, and I ask that You touch them with Your healing hand and restore them to wholeness. I pray that you heal the physical, emotional, and spiritual wounds that they are experiencing and that you bring them a sense of peace and restoration. In Jesus' name, I pray. Amen.

Prayer for Strength:
Heavenly Father, I pray for those dealing with trauma and

ask that you give them the strength they need to face each day. Lord, you know the weight that they are carrying, and I pray that you will give them the courage to keep moving forward. Please provide them with the strength to face their fears and the hope to know that they can overcome this trauma with your help. In Jesus' name, I pray. Amen.

Prayer for Peace:
Dear God, I pray for those dealing with trauma and ask that you bring them a sense of peace. Lord, I know that their hearts and minds are filled with worry and anxiety, and I ask that you calm their fears and give them a sense of tranquility. Please help them to find rest and peace in you and to know that you are in control. In Jesus' name, I pray. Amen.

Prayer for Guidance:
Heavenly Father, I pray for those dealing with trauma and ask that you guide them in the right direction. Lord, they are facing a difficult and uncertain road, and I ask that you give them wisdom and discernment as they navigate this journey. Please help them to know the steps to take and the decisions to make and to trust in your guidance and provision. In Jesus' name, I pray. Amen.

Reflection (Day 1)

Reflection (Day 2)

Reflection (Day 3)

Reflection (Day 4)

Reflection (Day 5)

Reflection (Day 6)

Reflection (Day 7)

Reflection (Day 8)

Reflection (Day 9)

Reflection (Day 10)

Reflection (Day 11)

Reflection (Day 12)

Reflection (Day 13)

Reflection (Day 14)

Reflection (Day 15)

Reflection (Day 16)

Reflection (Day 17)

Reflection (Day 18)

_____

_____

_____

_____

_____

_____

_____

_____

_____

_____

_____

_____

_____

_____

_____

Reflection (Day 19)

Reflection (Day 20)

Reflection (Day 21)

Reflection (Day 22)

Reflection (Day 23)

Reflection (Day 24)

Reflection (Day 25)

Reflection (Day 26)

Reflection (Day 27)

Reflection (Day 28)

Reflection (Day 29)

Reflection (Day 30)

www.ingramcontent.com/pod-product-compliance
Lightning Source LLC
Chambersburg PA
CBHW041132110526
44592CB00020B/2774